CANYON MEMORIES
BY VICTOR H. LYTLE

Vic Lytle at Rainbow Bridge

ISBN 968-7919-00-0

Original cover by Howard Jorgenson

THIS BOOK IS DEDICATED TO
TAYLOR T. HICKS D.D.S.
FRIEND AND HIKING COMPANION
(June 15, 1909 - June 26, 1988)

TABLE OF CONTENTS

INTRODUCTION

emories are fleeting things. Sometimes they play tricks on you. They blend in and out, giving a composite picture of two or more experiences. For example: my mind conjures up the memory of Roaring Springs on the North Kaibab Trail and blends it with the beautiful water gushing from the canyon wall at Thunder River Springs. Since I did not keep a diary, these recollections should not be considered factual source material.

Grand Canyon railroad station, early twenties

Looking at photographs has refreshed my memories, but even with these visual aids, I may not be able to put a name with a face, or trail with the proper ridge or drainage. Sometimes I draw a blank as to who my companions were on a certain trip. The slight is not intentional. The trails that are highlighted on the national park map are the ones I have traversed, sometimes more than once. The smaller fifteen minute maps give more detail.

My first remembrance of the Grand Canyon was a trip made with my parents in the early 1920's in a Reo touring car. I hesitate to say this, but at the early age of ten or eleven, my memories were more taken up with the experience of getting there than with the magnificence of a Natural Wonder of the World. Traveling up the old Black Canyon Road from Phoenix, took us two days to get to Prescott. Then fording Big Chino Wash after waiting a couple of hours for the flood waters to recede was an event of some consequence. All the cars waiting to cross cooperated, using a tow rope and the assembled manpower to pull each car across the muddy torrent. Making camp in the rain north of Williams turned out to be a needless inconvenience. The next morning as we were driving on to the Canyon, we found out that it hadn't rained a couple of miles up the road.

I am sure we must have seen the usual tourist views, but the only photographic record I have is a photograph of the railroad station, much as it looks today.

My next exposure to the Canyon was 14 years later when two college friends, Harry Bigger and Don Main, visited me in Prescott. This time as a tourist, I took photos from nearly all the view points but didn't venture below the rim. We stood in awe of this immense panorama of high plateaus and deep valleys.

Don Main and Harry Bigger 1935

I HAVASUPAI

ou might say that I really began to get acquainted with the Canyon when a family group rode horseback into the Havasupai Village in the summer of 1951.

The party included Robert E. Perkins, Medora Krieger, her daughter Katherine and a niece, my wife Ethel, and daughter Betty. It

Havasupai Falls

was a far cry from the crowds that descend upon the little bit of paradise today. The local natives were friendly but shy. Their houses were little more than windbreaks and little more was required for their moderate year-round climate. For tourists accommodations, we slept and ate in the government dispensary. I don't know what we would have done if there had been some one requiring medical attention. The Bureau of Indian Affairs agent (a non-Indian) took care of the logistics and saw that horses were ready when required, and collected the fees, which were minimal.

We rode from the Village past the Navajo Falls and Havasupai Falls. What a magnificent sight the beautiful blue-green water was plunging over the travertine cliffs. The third and highest of the three was Mooney Falls, supposed to be higher than Niagara Falls. Along the banks of the streams was quite a lot of plant growth, including one called wild celery. More about that later.

We all had a refreshing swim, but were warned not to drink the water in the stream. Everyone was taking pictures of this beautiful green valley nestled at the foot of the giant red sandstone walls. On top of these sandstone walls were two tall columns that looked as if a good strong wind would blow them over. One was supposedly a good God and the other a bad God. Tradition has it that when and if these sandstone monoliths fall, the Havasupai people will be no more. I am sure that some of the earth movements caused by underground nuclear testing going on in nearby Nevada must have given the natives cause for concern.

As we prepared to ride out, Ethel came down with dysentery that made the ride out a bit unpleasant for her. She surmised that it was caused by eating wild celery at Mooney Falls.

It was on this trip that I began to view with awe the magnitude of the Canyon.

I was determined that my plans for the future would be to come back and explore more of it.

Betty Perkins at Havasupai Hilltop

II Rainbow Bridge

Have you ever noticed that when a dentist gets your mouth full of tools and sponges, he starts asking you questions? That was my situation when Dr. Taylor Hicks Sr. asked me if I would be interested in backpacking into Rainbow Bridge. What could I say?

Rainbow Bridge

He took my silence as consent and started briefing me about plans for food and equipment. Our group consisted of Dr. Hicks, his son Paul, Leland Marsh (who later met his death at night on the North Kaibab Trail), Aulton Jones, finance officer at the Prescott Veterans Administration Center, Dick Carter of the Camera Center, and myself.

We were to leave Thursday afternoon March 27, 1957 and drive to Rainbow Lodge where we would make camp and be ready for an early start down the trail to the bridge on Friday morning. It was a 14 mile hike. At the last minute, Dick Carter had a conflicting engagement that kept him from leaving with us Thursday. He flew up Friday morning with a friend, "Pas" Kuhn, in his Piper Cub. Pas said he knew of a little landing strip at Rainbow Lodge.

Our trip was uneventful except for gasoline problems. We were planning to fill up with gas at Tonalea so we would have plenty to get to Rainbow Lodge and back.

However, the trading post was closed as was the one at Cow Springs. We calculated we could make it to the lodge and back. There was no paved road after Tuba City, and the last quarter mile was washed out, eroded sandstone and was like driving down the Prescott Court House steps. We had not made as good time as we had anticipated. It was

dark by the time we finished eating. The lodge had burned down a few years before so the only shelters were some locked tent houses. It was turning cold and looked stormy. Paul and Leland found a way to get into one of the tent houses. Aulton and I joined them when it started a light drizzle. Taylor, being a true outdoors man, opted to bed down in a protected spot in the corner of two remaining walls of the burned-out trading post. When we awoke Friday morning, Taylor had an additional blanket - about 4 inches of snow.

We had spotted the air strip on the way in. After eating we packed all our gear and drove back to the air strip to meet Dick at 8:00 a.m. Soon we heard the plane's engine but saw that they were circling quite some distance to the south. We decided to attract their attention by building a fire and putting some sage brush on it to make more smoke. It did the job and soon they were on the ground with us. Only one problem. Pas didn't think he had enough gas to get back to Tuba City. We didn't have any to spare in the station wagon. Pas said there was some residual fuel in the wing tank. The only container we had was a quart thermos bottle which we used to drain the wing tanks and put in the main tank. Pas was off then in a bee line for Tuba City. By the time we were ready to hit the trail, it was ten o'clock.

Dick Carter was the least prepared for the hike either as to physical fitness or equipment. After an hour or so on the trail, we could determine that he wasn't going to make it. The weight of his camera equipment alone would have been quite a load.

It was decided that he should turn back and wait for us to return on Sunday. Dick said he would give a thousand dollars for a horse, whereupon around the next bend, as if on cue, came an Indian and his squaw on horseback. They put Dick on the squaw's horse and took him back to camp. We heard later that the fee was settled for a pocket knife and a pair of socks.

Aulton and I were not in the best of shape either. By the time we had crossed Red Bud Pass, we were falling behind. As it started to get dark we yelled to the others that we were going to sack out along the trail and would see them in the morning. We were so tired we didn't even prepare our dinner, just spread out our sleeping bags and crawled in. I remarked to Aulton, "What I wouldn't give for a nice cool drink right now." Within a few minutes, someone appeared out of the gloom and asked, "Who wanted a drink?" Unbeknown to us, we had stopped near the entrance to the campground where there was a nice spring. A wrangler with his two guests had overheard my remark and obliged me with a cup of clear cool water. Was I surprised!

Earlier, the lady from the other group was equally surprised, sitting in a campground outhouse with the door open

Paul and Leland on top of the bridge

facing the trail as the other three members of our party walked by. She had come in on a horse from Navajo Mountain Trading Post and didn't think there was anyone within 20 miles. She and her husband, both M.D.'s from Washington D.C., didn't realize

there was another trail in from Rainbow Lodge.

On Saturday, Taylor, Aulton and I decided to hike on down to the Colorado River, about 8 miles round trip, while Paul and Leland stayed at the bridge. On the way back, the sun was hot and we couldn't resist skinny dipping in a nice cool pool. When we got back to camp, Paul and Leland were on top of the bridge.

We hiked out as far as the last possible water and made camp so we would not have so far to go on Sunday. Out on top with Dick there waiting for us, we were soon loaded and ready to go. We planned to gas up at one of the trading posts but Cow Springs was still closed for the Easter weekend as was Red Lake and Tonalea. Their fuel was trucked in by 55 gallon drums. When we couldn't raise anyone, we examined all the barrels hoping to find a few residual gallons. No luck!

Nothing to do but go on as far as we could go. About 10 miles down the road, we had had it. The road was just a doublebarreled cow trail and no traffic but a couple of Indian ponies, which Paul and Leland tried to rope. The first car that came along stopped. It was a couple of Indians in a pickup. No one had a tow rope or cable. We were finally able to make a close connection with our tire chains. Away we went. The Indian chose to use the two ruts in the middle to travel on. He had only two speeds - full throttle ahead or none. He chose full throttle with dust and rocks flying all around us. We couldn't have seen an oncoming vehicle if there had been one. I actually hoped the chain would break. What a wild ride!

When we came to the pavement about 2 miles from Tuba City, he slowed down to about 5 miles an hour. After filling his truck and ours with gas, we headed for home with only a stop in Flagstaff for a hamburger.

Despite the transportation problems, the trip was a memorable one, and I was hooked on backpacking in the canyons of the Colorado.

RAINBOW BRIDGE — 1958
Notes for Next Year

✓ FRIDAY BREAKFAST —

  ✓ BACON & EGGS —
    COFFEE — TOAST — FRUIT

FRIDAY NOON —

    SANDWICHES — FRUIT — COOKIES

FRIDAY NITE —   SOUP 1/2
    HAMBURGER — Mashed POTATOES
    COFFEE — FRUIT (PEACHES)

SATURDAY MORNING
    SPAM & EGGS
      COFFEE — FRUIT (APPLE SAUCE)

SATURDAY NOON —
      SOUP & SPAM — FRUIT (APPLESAUCE)
      MILK

SATURDAY NITE —
      SOUP & CASAROLE — FRUIT (APP
      TEA

SUNDAY MORNING: —
      COFFEE — BACON — SOUP 1/2

SUNDAY NOON: —
      SOUP — MILK

18

Policy No.	Amount	Premium	Expires

SUNDAY EVENING :
   SOUP — SPAM SANDWICHES
   FRESH ORANGES —
   COOKIES — COFFEE

TO LEAVE IN CAR :
1. BLANKET & PILLOW
2. SHOVEL — TARP.
3. COOLER — SOFT DRINKS
4. WATER CAN —
5. ICE BOX — DRY ICE
     BACON — EGGS — HAMBURGER
     BREAD — ORANGES

6. CHAP STICK
7 SWEAT SHIRTS

52   Sugar & Salt
  23   MEASURING CUP
 156   PLYERS
104   TIN CAN
1196
  598   Carnation Milk
        Bread & Butter

19

III Ribbon Falls

Spring is the time to hike in the Grand Canyon. The days are not too hot and the nights are not too cold. Most of the snow has melted and if there is a spring indicated on the map, it is generally running. Hence most of our hikes were tied in with the schools Easter breaks, as was our hike in the spring of 1960. The previous year my brother's four children came to live with us. We added two more boys of junior high age to our family and I figured that backpacking would be a change for all of us. John invited school friend Laurie Smith, and Norman brought Robin Waples. Jim, Bob, and I rounded out the predominantly family group.

Laurie Smith, Robin Waples, Jim Lytle, John Lytle

We left after school one Thursday and spent that night in the campgrounds on the South Rim. It is hard to believe today that on

21

an Easter weekend we were not required to have reservations at any of the campgrounds at the rim or in the Canyon itself. In fact, we were not required to stay in designated campgrounds and we could still build fires for cooking or warmth.

In the morning as the sun started to weave its tapestry of lights and shadows on the canyon walls, I began my first descent below the rim of the Grand Canyon. When you walk through a man-made arch about 400 yards from the rim and start your first switchback, you realize that you are part of the Canyon - a very insignificant part. There are very few places where wind, water and earth movement have made it possible to find a place to fit a trail, hence most of the foot traffic and mule trains use the Bright Angel Trail or the Kaibab Trail. The trails are wide and well maintained.

After descending through the limestone and sandstone formations, we came upon a little oasis called Indian Gardens where a Park Ranger lives among the cottonwood trees. The spring here has for many years been the principal source of water for the village on the South Rim. We didn't tarry long there. One can take a side trip there to Plateau Point where you can get a good view of the Inner Gorge without hiking down to it.

Our trail followed the creek in a gradual descent to the Colorado River with just a couple of switch backs to take us around waterfalls. Nearly always, one sees Mule Deer in this vicinity and this day was no exception. As we descended further into the Inner Gorge, we were to lose our view of the greater canyon. The granite walls seemed quite confining.

Bridge over the Colorado River

up over the years. We camped here for the night; in fact, two of the boys bedded down in a cove behind the falls. With a long hike behind us and the soothing sound of the waterfall, it didn't take us long to get to sleep.

Ribbon Falls

Our trail took us upstream to the footbridge, the only crossing in about 300 miles. There is a nice campground here at the confluence of Bright Angel Creek and the Colorado. After a short rest, we followed this babbling brook for 4 more miles to Ribbon Falls, which as the name implies is a small volume of water plunging about 100 feet to a travertine deposit that it has built

There were a few sore muscles the next morning, but with breakfast out of the way, we broke camp and started retracing our steps.

Bright Angel Creek between Ribbon Falls and Phantom Ranch. Jim and John Lytle

It made the trip back to Indian Gardens seem like a breeze. We shared the campground with a couple of other groups.

Our hike on Easter morning was one to remember with the sun lighting up the Redwall and the Coconino Sandstone. It was easy to understand why so many people come to participate in the Easter sunrise worship service held each year on the point. As we came up the trail, we could hear the voices of the choir. What a beautiful Easter morning!

It was now all downhill, and with the sun lighting the canyon cliffs, and the cool clear stream besides us, who could ask for anything more?

When we got to Phantom Ranch, we found out the management allowed hikers to use the swimming pool and the dressing rooms. What a pleasant break.

Swimming pool Phantom Ranch

24

IV THUNDER RIVER

March 30-April 2, 1961

For our Thunder River hike in the Spring of 1961, we did quite a bit of advance planning. We wrote letters to the Kaibab National Forest; to Jonreed Lauritzen, author of many articles about the Grand Canyon; to Harvey Butchart, the font of all knowledge about the Canyon; and to Carl Cox, owner or the Kaibab Lodge on the North Rim. Making this trip, in addition to our veteran hiker, Dr. Taylor Hicks, were the Lytle boys, Norman, John, Jim, Bob, and Norman's friend Robin Waples.

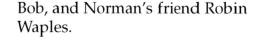

North Kaibab Trail

The North Rim is a long trip from Prescott - 415 miles to be exact. Our destination for the first night was Big Saddle Camp. It was a good thing that we brought extra blankets for the first night. We bedded down in a cabin used by hunters and foresters as it was really cold. With two feet of snow on the ground, it was impossible to go any further and it was another 14 miles up Indian Hollow Road to the trail head. Harvey Butchart had told Taylor of a game trail off Crazy Jug Point that would connect with the main trail. The game trail was just that and it soon disappeared, as the wild animals went their separate ways. We were following rock cairns and contour maps and didn't intercept the main trail until late afternoon.

There was some fresh water from recent rain in potholes in the rocks. We decided to make camp even though we had planned to get all the way to Thunder Springs our first day, and we had only made it about halfway.

In the morning we decided to leave our packs and hike in and out in one day. I even had time to make a few casts for trout in Thunder River, but no luck. Thunder Springs was even more beautiful than expected.

Trail marker on the trail to Thunder River
Bob and Jim Lytle

Thunder Springs

I had never before seen such a large volume of water bursting forth from a rock, crystal clear and cold.

Thunder Springs

We had heard there was a trail over to Deer Creek Falls, but we didn't have time to pursue it. That would have to wait for another time. The view of Surprise Valley looked enticing too. The magnitude of the Canyon is something that never fails to impress the first time hiker or for that matter the seasoned veteran of this mighty chasm. Take one square mile any place in the Canyon and move it anywhere else in the country and you will have a significant national monument.

Unusual rock formation on Thunder River Trail

When you consider how many square miles there are in the Grand Canyon and its tributaries, you just can't put it in perspective. We got back to our campsite in time to enjoy the changing colors of the canyon walls.

While preparing our evening meal, we started making plans for the hike out the next day. We could follow the contours better on the way out, which saved time and energy by avoiding climbing in and out of a myriad of steep drainages.

Shortly after we had started up the trail, I was bringing up the rear with Bob just ahead of me. He was doing quite well for a seven year-old. He carried his own pack, learning early to carry only that which was really necessary. I noticed that he kept scratching his back. I asked if his pack was bothering him. He said, "No", he had been bothered by mosquitoes last night. I hadn't noticed any insects during the night so we decided to have a look. When we shed his pack and rolled up his shirt, we found that he had a full-blown case of chicken pox. There was not much we could do, but we all took turns carrying his pack to the top. There we made a bed for him in the back of the station wagon.

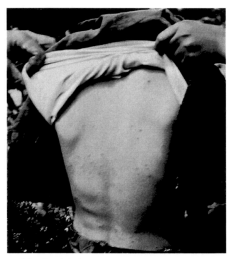

Bobby's chicken pox

On our way out of the Kaibab Forest, we saw lots of wild game: deer, elk, turkey, and of course the well-known Kaibab Squirrel with its white bushy tail that provides camouflage when snow covers the ground. We also had heard of mountain lion in the area and had seen the cabin where President

Teddy Roosevelt stayed while lion hunting. When we stopped for dinner at Parry's Lodge in Kanab, Utah, Jim glanced at the menu and announced that he was going to have a lion steak. The waitress was quick to point out that the menu said loin steak.

I can't remember where we stopped to spend the night, but the long drive up to the North Rim had been well worth it to see another beautiful part of the Canyon, and to experience hiking without the benefit of a trail. Our use of contour maps was going to stand us in good stead on later hikes.

Vic relaxing on the hike out

V RAINBOW BRIDGE

April 19-23, 1962

When word got around town that we were talking about another hike into Rainbow Bridge, there were quite a number of families and friends that wanted to be included. The final group included my nephew, Wally Patterson, an electrical engineer at General Electric in Phoenix; Abia Judd, Superintendent of Prescott Public Schools, and his sons, Whitney and Eric; Howard Jorgenson, retired Air Force Colonel and his son Tim; Waldo Bast, science teacher at the high school; the Lytle tribe, John, Jim, and Bob, plus Pat Shire - a friend of John's; and repeaters from our first trip; Dr. Taylor Hicks, Aulton Jones, and me. Two of the group were ten years-old and one sixty with varying degrees of physical fitness.

Rainbow Bridge

We got started a little earlier and could go at a slower pace than the first trip. Starting from the Navajo

Plateau, the trail descended gradually through piñon and sagebrush until we reached a steeper descent with a spectacular view. The boys nicknamed it Yarnell Hill. We soon reached an area of huge boulders. The imagination of the hikers ran wild as they saw the likenesses of bears, elephants, birds, etc. We knew that we had to get from the drainage we were in to the one that the bridge was in.

Shadow Arch

The identifying landmark was a shadow arch on the left hand wall of the canyon. The shadow arch gives one a clue as to how the rainbow arch was formed. It was a perfect rainbow in bas relief but still attached to the canyon wall.

Red Bud Pass

Our trail now took a sharp right turn up a narrow defile called Red Bud Pass that is as steep as any we encountered. It was loose red sand, where you took two steps forward and slid back one. It was the most physically demanding part of the trail. We all made it with a few rest stops.

Red Bud Pass

Confluence of the Colorado River and Aztec Creek. Aztec Point is now under Lake Powell

We were now in Aztec Canyon, and it wasn't long before we came to running water. Waldo Bast and the Judd family had developed sore feet. Since there were still a few miles to go, they decided to make camp and make the rest of the trek into the bridge and back the next day without their packs.

It was well worth the added effort to continue to the bridge and see it in the changing lights and shadows.

It is customary for each hiker to carry his own food, but several would share a cooking fire. As the sun went down it was a peaceful sight to see the groups sitting around their little fires. Someone would throw more wood on one of the fires and then we would review the day's activities. Soon someone would prevail on Taylor to sing "Little Joe the Wrangler" or one of his repertoire of western cowboy songs. One by one the hikers left the circle of light and

On the trail to Rainbow Bridge

crawled into their sleeping bags. I didn't go to sleep right away as I couldn't take my eyes off the spectacular sight of the bridge in the light of a full moon.

The next day Taylor, Alton and I did a repeat trip to the Colorado River, joined by son Jim. We knew about how long it would take us this time, so we took time to study the beauty of the Canyon's precipitous Redwall 500 feet high and the sculpturing of wind and water over the centuries. In some places it was less than 50 feet wide. It would be hard to accept the Big Bang Theory of Evolution here.

When we returned to the bridge we decided to go back to the last

34

water and make camp with the rest of our party. This shortened the hike out the next day. The moon was so bright after we finished eating that John and Pat Shire talked us into letting them hike out by moonlight. As I look back on it. I probably made a poor decision as many things could have happened to them. It turned out they had no problems and it is something they shall never forget. They were at Rainbow Lodge to meet us the next morning. It was a memorable trip, especially for those who hiked down to the river, for the next time we were to see the bridge, the trail to the Colorado would be submerged in 200 feet of water backed up by the Glen Canyon Dam. But that is another story.

Sunrise at Rainbow Lodge

VI HAVASUPAI

In November of 1962 was the first time we journeyed into the Canyon in the fall of the year. On rather short notice, Colonel Jorgenson and son Tim joined Jim, Bob, and me for a weekend at Havasupai.

We left our car at the Hilltop where a few other cars were parked, some of which looked like they hadn't been moved in some

Howard Jorgenson, Bob and Jim Lytle at Havasupai Falls

time and probably belonged to the residents of the village. As it turned out, we were the only visitors who were backpacking into the canyon. There was one small group going in on horseback.

The trail starts out down a few steep switchbacks then levels out and follows a dry creek bed the rest of the way, not a very sensational trek.

When we finally came to the live creek from Havasu Springs, it was a different story. The deciduous trees were decked out in their fall colors and the fields were still green. The blue-green water was like a turquoise ribbon holding it all together. We didn't linger long at the village, but went past Navajo Falls and on to the camp ground just below Havasupai Falls where there is a bubbling spring that isn't highly mineralized like the stream.

The next morning while Bob and the Jorgensons explored a side canyon where there had been some mining activity at one time, Jim and I hiked down to the Colorado River. We had calculated that it would take most of the day to hike to the river and back so we took a sandwich along for lunch. Our first challenge was the descent around Mooney Falls which is said to be higher than Niagara Falls. The spray from the falls made the trail quite slippery in places. Someone had driven some steel rods into the rocks for hand holds that were really a great help. I think this was the first time I had ever been in an area that no grazing animal (wild or domestic) could reach. The high canyon walls proved an effective barrier. There wasn't a maintained trail, so we just meandered back and forth from one side of the creek to the other.

Jim in creek crossing

At first we stopped to take off our boots and levis each time we crossed, but that proved too time consuming. So we just sloshed across the creek from that time on in our boots. In one place the water was up to our armpits.

One of the most beautiful sites was Beaver Falls, a side canyon with a small stream plunging down travertine terraces.

At each turn in the canyon, we would think that surely the Colorado would just be around the next bend. The first clue was not visual but audible. While still in the narrow canyon and unable to see out, we could hear the roar of the mighty river. When we finally reached the confluence of the two streams, we were about 10 or 15 feet above where the blue-green water mixed with the red.

Beaver Falls

Confluence of Havasu Creek and the Colorado River

39

There was no easy access to the rivers edge. After nine crossings of the cold stream, lying in the sun on the warm rocks was just what we needed. We didn't do much more than eat our soggy sandwiches and start back. It had taken us four hours to come down and we didn't relish the thought of climbing around Mooney Falls after dark and with no flashlight. We made it with a little daylight to spare. No long stories around the campfire that night. We were ready to crawl into our sleeping bags as soon as dinner was cleaned up.

We took it easy on our hike out the next day, taking pictures and savoring our last view of the little Shangri-La!

VII RIBBON FALLS

April 11-14, 1963

By the spring of 1963, I was involved in Boy Scouting with Troop 1, sponsored by the First Congregational Church. I was assistant scout master. Some of the senior scouts needed some overnight hikes to complete their hiking merit badge work. We decided to do a repeat of our 1960 hike to Ribbon Falls. I persuaded Dr. Hicks and Alton Jones to come along to give the scouts the benefit of their backpacking experiences. From Troop 1, were Paul Ridenhour, Richard Campbell, Bob Cook, Marc Burhans, Howard Balentine, Jim and Bob Lytle.

Ribbon Falls

All of the scouts had to have participated in some conditioning hikes up Granite Mountain, Thumb Butte and Spruce Mountain. I made an exception for one boy who had missed one of the hikes due to a conflicting junior high scheduled football game. I figured his conditioning for sports would be sufficient to see him through.

We took the Bright Angel Trail even though it is a little longer than the Kaibab. The fact that there are a couple of springs on this trail is also a plus. I found that I didn't get as much time to enjoy the beauty of the Canyon when the responsibility for six boys rested squarely on my shoulders. No one seemed to have any problems. We stopped for a snack at Indian Gardens.

The muddy Colorado River

connect with the South Kaibab Trail, just before crossing on the foot bridge at Bright Angel Campgrounds. We were all ready for a swim by the time we reached Phantom Ranch.

View from Bright Angel Trail

Continuing our downward trek, we stopped again when we reached the muddy Colorado. When following the river you have a slight upgrade before you

Bob Lytle at Phantom Ranch

42

Pleasantly refreshed, we took off for Ribbon Falls. Everyone moved right along except for one boy whose tail was dragging. You guessed it - the football player. He just couldn't keep up. I had to see that he got to the campsite. I pushed, I pulled, I cajoled, I threatened, I did everything but carry him or his pack. He was a good physical specimen but he just wasn't in shape. The rest of the troop were busy exploring Ribbon Falls by the time I got Richard into camp.

Some had even discovered the trail to the upper falls - a beautiful sight but not as spectacular as the lower area. After supper, Taylor entertained us with "Tying a Knot in the Devil's Tail" and other songs and stories. Then all was quiet. As I lay looking at the sky, the transcontinental airplane lights were visible on their way to the west coast, but the plane was high enough that no sounds were audible.

Ribbon Falls

Bright Angel Canyon

In the morning it seemed like the sun would never break over the canyon wall and give us some direct rays to warm us up. Most of the trail was on the east side of Bright Angel creek so that we were in the shade till almost noon. At Phantom Ranch there was a little snack bar where you could purchase candy bars and other snacks for the trail. They really tasted good after a diet of dehydrated food for two days. As we were hiking along the river bank back to Indian Gardens, five or six deer came down to the river to drink.

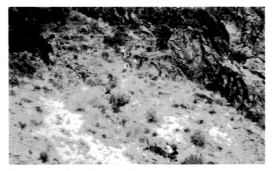

Deer crossing the trail

They weren't exactly wild but they kept an eye on us as we continued on the trail.

One would think that those hiking into the Canyon would be the only ones enjoying the spectacular views. The upward bound hikers have changed scenes also. When you break out of the Inner Gorge onto the Tonto Plateau, you have the challenging walls facing you without any discernible trail in sight and the Park Service intends to keep it that way.

Indian Gardens is a pleasant place to camp but there is generally enough air movement that you had better have everything battened down or it won't be there next morning. One of the boys lost a hat and another found his tin plate about 25 yards down stream.

The hike out from Indian Gardens isn't as demanding as some other trails. As usual I was "Tailend Charlie." My pack was weighing a little more than the customary 45 pounds. The young strong boys were probably a half hour ahead of me. My son Jim did what became a tradition, leaving his pack on top, and coming back down the trail for my pack. Dirty as we were, we all went into the Harvey House for a bowl of chili before heading home.

Left to right: Richard Campbell, Paul Ridenhour, Jim Lytle, Mark Burhans, Twig Branch, Taylor Hicks, Bob Lytle, Alton Jones, Howard Balentine

VIII HAVASUPAI FALLS

 soon found out that it was easier and wiser to take the scout troop on hikes that some of the leaders had already experienced. In March of 1964, Troop 1 was ready for Havasupai. But so were lots of other people. I didn't keep a list of the ones who made the trek. I imagine there were ten or twelve. The relative ease of the trail made it possible for the group to get

Havasupai Village

strung out over quite a distance as we started down Havasupai Trail. The senior scouts who were leading the way stopped at the village to wait for the slower ones. There was no camping fee for scouts but they did collect a dollar from everyone with a camera. There was quite a number of people at the campground so we moved on up Carbonate Canyon where we could be together as a group. This side canyon enters Supai Canyon from the east about midway between Supai Falls and Mooney Falls and had been the site of some mining activity at one time.

The campground was beginning to show the effects of unrestricted use. Dry wood was scarce and some people had even stripped green branches from the trees. Thank goodness they hadn't defaced the Canyon walls.

The main attraction for the boys the next day was swimming under the Supai Falls. A few hikers ventured as far as Beaver Falls but none were interested in going on to the Colorado River.

Mooney Falls

The hike out the following day presented no problems. It is always with regret that one leaves this little piece of paradise. The desert seems dryer and the trail a little steeper. I hold that last look in special remembrance until we journey this way again. Most of the water for Havasu Creek comes from Havasu Springs and it is a common mistake to follow the water to the left up Havasu Canyon instead of taking the right hand trail up Hualapai Canyon which is nearly always dry and leads back to Hilltop where we had left our cars.

IX RAINBOW BRIDGE

With the filling of Lake Powell behind Glen Canyon Dam a new dimension was added to backpacking into Rainbow Bridge and Glen Canyon. We planned a new approach for the Easter trek in April of 1964. Two fine Prescott citizens, John Jackson, and J.R. Williams made their boats and their skill as pilots available to Boy Scout Troop 1. One half of the troop under the leadership

On the trail to Rainbow Bridge

of Dr. Hicks and Conrad Brekke hiked from Rainbow Lodge into the bridge and went out by boat. The other half under my leadership with the help of Marshal Beebe (Captain U.S. Navy-retired) came in by boat from the marina and hiked out. Bob Cook furnished transportation to Wahweap, but didn't participate in the boating or hiking. Jim Lytle had a broken ankle after planing to take the trip, so he went on a round trip boat ride. The lake was far from being full and the boats couldn't go up Bridge Canyon much beyond the mount of Forbidden Canyon. It was just a short hike up from there to the bridge. The two groups exchanged greetings and car keys and proceeded on their respective journeys.

Boating on Lake Powell

The itinerary had been planned so that the group that hiked in would be able to drive home on Saturday and be in attendance in church on Sunday for Easter services. But the best laid schemes of mice an' men "gang aft a gley". There wasn't a marina at the bridge in those days. One had to carry enough gasoline for the round trip. On the return trip they were still quite a ways from Wahweap and bucking head winds they noticed that both boats were running low on fuel. They decided to put all the remaining gas in one boat and leave one boat and the scouts and their gear to spend the night on a sand bar in Lake Powell. With the lighter load and added fuel they made it to Wahweap. Next morning they returned to the abandoned group with sufficient fuel for all to get back to Wahweap, all be it a day later than planned.

Meanwhile, back at the bridge the "Hike out bunch" having signed the guest register on Saturday, taken pictures and explored the side canyons decided to hike out as far as Redbud Creek to shorten the trek on Sunday. It also gave us a chance to maintain a more leisurely pace and enjoy the beauties of the area.

Shortly after we hit the trail Sunday, we took a rest stop and had a short Easter religious service lead by Bob Cook and Tommy Robbins. After experiencing the bustle of the tourists at the bridge, it was a relief to have a quiet time in this natural amphitheater.

On the trail from Rainbow Bridge

The remainder of the journey was a gradual transition from sand stone walls to high desert plateau with juniper and piñon pine. One cannot hike in the Rainbow Bridge country without feeling the dominating presence of Navajo Mountain.

It isn't its height (a little over 10,000 feet) but its mass - a good bearing point when you become disoriented. It would be a challenging hike with the permission of the Navajo people.

Snow covered Navajo Mountain

X GRANDVIEW TO HORSESHOE MESA

March 18-20, 1966

In the spring of 1966 we decided it was time to explore some of the unmaintained trails. The Grandview Trail was our first choice. Easter week (March 18) was early and stormy weather was forecast. Regardless, we decided to give it a try.

Wayne Price a CPA was helping with Troop 1. We took five senior scouts- Howard Ballentine, Paul Ridenhour, Dennis Price, Jim

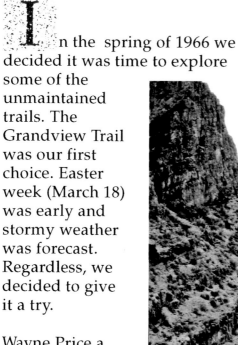

Grandview Trail with snow

Lytle, and Elroy Dornick.When we arrived at Grand View Point on the south rim of the Grand Canyon, it was snowing and blowing. We decided to hike down the trail and lose about a thousand feet of elevation to get out of the snow. The precipitation had changed to a light rain and soon stopped altogether. Our campsites weren't the best. There was barely room for the seven sleeping bags along side

53

the trail among the rocks, piñons and the junipers. It was not a place for sleep walking.

We weren't concerned about other hikers on the trail as we were the only crazies around.

The morning broke bright and clear. I could in my sleeping bag look straight down for about 500 feet! Grandview Trail was originally a tourist trail

Grandview Trail

for hotel guests. There had ben some major construction projects literally hanging the trail to the face of the canyon wall. It didn't seem precarious as you descended,but when you looked back you wondered how long it was going to be before it would need major maintenance or replacement.

It didn't take long to get to Horseshoe Mesa which as the name implies was a horseshoe shaped formation on the Tonto Plateau. About midway along the west side of the mesa a cave was discovered on our right. We hadn't come equipped to do any exploring, but using our flashlights we penetrated the darkness for a couple of hundred yards. It was not a wet cave, in fact it was quite dusty.

No stalagmites or stalactites in the area we explored.

We backtracked to the junction with east Grandview Trail and ate lunch in a deserted mining cabin. The air was cool and crisp but it was delightful sitting in out of the breeze. We had no trouble reaching our planned destination following Cottonwood Creek drainage to Cottonwood Spring and Campground.

We had been told that there was a trail to the Colorado River at this point. We found rock cairns that indicated the decent but the trail was not too apparent. We didn't think we had enough daylight left to find our way in and out to the river. So we returned to our campsite for supper and a pleasant evening around the campfire.

By morning the storm clouds moved on and we enjoyed excellent hiking conditions. We retraced our steps following the Cottonwood Creek Trail to the East Grandview Trail where we took a short rest at the old mining cabin.

Mining cabin Horseshoe Mesa

We had toyed with the idea of going down the east fork of the trail to Page Springs to replenish our water supply. Knowing that we would encounter snow on the upper parts of our trail, we forged ahead. We had about 2,500 vertical feet to climb and four or five miles of hiking.

Sure enough we found knee-deep snow on the final switch backs. It was powder snow and hadn't been packed down. It wasn't icy or slippery. It was just the extra effort of lifting your feet that made it slow going. We all agreed it would make an excellent hike for the entire troop.

View of the Colorado River

XI Hiking to Phantom Ranch to Take a Colorado Raft Trip

April 7-17, 1966

In April of 1966 we again had a Canyon experience that combined hiking and boating. Taylor Hicks told us that he had signed up for a raft trip down the Colorado River from Lees Ferry to Temple Bar on Lake Mead where we would spend the night. We, Jim, Bob and I were a little late in getting reservations and had to settle for a shorter trip joining

Georgie White raft trip down the Colorado River

Taylor at Phantom Ranch and finishing at Temple Bar. All our gear went by mule from Grand Canyon Village to Phantom Ranch. Thus relieved of heavy packs, we decided to explore the Tonto Trail from Grandview to the Kaibab Trail. This time it was just Jim, Bob and me. Ethel and Frances Hicks had delivered us to Moqui Lodge just outside the national park. Our hike plans called for us to take day packs and lunch and hitch hike to Grandview Point to leave there at 8:00 a.m. and arrive at Phantom Ranch in time for a steak dinner with our rafting group.

We got a ride with the first car to come along. Fortunately for us it was some specialized workmen doing the welding on the new

Jim and Bob Lytle by century plant Bast Tonto Trail

aluminum pipe line from Roaring Springs to Grand Canyon Village whose contract called for their time to start when they left the motel. There was a helicopter to pick them up at Yaki Point and fly them to their work site. After hearing our plans they decided to take us out to our departure point at the head of Grandview. This undoubtedly saved us precious time and didn't bother them since they were being paid for their time, and the helicopter would wait for them.

There was no lingering to take in the view. We thought we were making good time when we reached Horseshoe Mesa at midmorning and continued down Cottonwood Creek. We took a short break at

Cottonwood Spring, and filled our canteens. We were now on the Tonto Plateau and faced our first major drainage - Grapevine Creek. We stopped for lunch at Grapevine Spring.

By midafternoon we realized that we had not allowed enough time to work around the drainages. It was 3:00 p.m. by the time we reached a point on Grapevine Canyon opposite the point where we had lunch. We pushed on loosing no time as we skirted Boulder Creek and Lone Tree Creek. Fortunately we had no water problems as all the springs shown on our contour map were live. We hiked until it got too dark to see the trail. Our flashlights were in our packs waiting for us at Bright Angel Creek. Jim, our "be prepared" scout reached in his jacket pocket and came up with a packet of dehydrated soup. We built a small cooking fire and nothing ever tasted better than that soup. We waited for the moon to come up at about 11:00 p.m. Following the trail by moonlight was complicated by many wild burro trails along the Tonto Rim. Shortly before we intersected the Kaibab Trail, we stopped for a breather. Bob turned to me and said "You don't think we are lost do you Pop?"

It wasn't long before the Kaibab Trail loomed up in the moonlight like a four lane highway. Mostly it gave us a sense of security as we had all hiked on it before. We learned later that after dinner Taylor had walked up to this point looking for us. It was 2:00 a.m. by the time we found our group bedded down on a sand bar near Bright Angel Creek. But we didn't have a clue as to where our duffel bags were. We just stretched out on the sand and were soon asleep. All we had missed were a few hours sleep and a steak dinner.

The group we joined was conducted by Georgie White - "Woman of the River".

Georgie White

Our raft was made of three war surplus pontoon bridges lashed together to accommodate about 30 people. Our gear was lashed down in the middle pontoon. Our only means of propulsion was a twenty horse power outboard motor which served as a rudder.

From here on we were going to be mainly on the water.

Some of the people were leaving the group at Phantom Ranch and walking out the Bright Angel Trail. Among this group was Bob Belt, a Prescott friend. He asked me where our rain suits were. It had been on the list of things to bring along but I didn't think it would be necessary as warm as it was at the floor of the Canyon in April. Bob insisted I take his and he found one for Bob Lytle. Jim had a slicker in his pack. I was very grateful as I was not aware how little sunshine gets into the Inner Gorge and how cold the river was.

We started out with a couple of relatively small rapids; Horn Creek and Hermit in which we got splashed a little. We got our first drenching at Crystal Rapids. It seemed like we were constantly wet from there on. A river trip is not the best way to get a complete view of the Canyon. The Inner Gorge is quite confining. You have to get up to the Tonto Plateau before you get a feeling of the immensity of the Canyon. We generally picked a nice sunny beach when we stopped for the night about four thirty or five o'clock. Georgie didn't allow drinking while on the river so we didn't have a cocktail hour. We had heard that some of the other outfitters did. She did allow a small measure of blackberry cordial which she provided. The Park Service was still allowing fires on the beaches and hadn't mandated porto-potties yet. So it was boys upstream and girls downstream.

The food was good and for our particular group, the food was furnished by the Kraft Food Co. They were introducing a new line of institutional foods and were going to use our activities for their promotional advertising.

The Kraft photographers took a great many pictures and offered copies of their slides to the people on the trip at no cost.

We generally made a midmorning stop. I can't remember them all but we made one at Elves Chasm, a beautiful travertine grotto where Royal Arch Creek plunged into the Colorado.

We made an overnight stop at Tapeats Creek.

Wading across Tapeats Creek on the way to Thunder River

The next morning we followed the creek up to Thunder Spring, which we had approached from the North Rim in 1961.

The flow of the spring and Thunder River which it forms, seem to maintain a constant flow into Tapeats Creek. After a light lunch, we made a few camera stops and returned to the raft. We made a short stop a Deer Creek Falls. It is possible to hike up Deer Creek by a trail that goes around the falls but we had to keep moving. We'd had one hike for the day which was enough for most of our party.

The next day we stopped where the blue-green waters of the Havasupai Creek merges with the Colorado. This was the only time we encountered another tourist group at one of our scenic stops. There isn't any beach so it was sort of a scramble up the rocks for those who ventured up the creek for a little ways. The 7 $^1/_2$ mile hike up to Havasu Village was not included in our trip.

Next came Lava Falls, the rapid we had all been waiting for.

Lava Falls

It is the result of an ancient lava flow blocking the river. We stopped above the rapid to make sure or gear was all secure and to give the photographers a chance to position themselves for the best possible shots. Georgie also wanted time to "read" the rapid which is constantly changing.

When all was ready we started our descent through Lava Falls.

we were sure we would crash but Georgie had been there before. At the last minute her maneuver sent us sliding down a tongue of the rapid. A few more bumps and we were through, soaking wet but ready to do it again. They said we had dropped 35 feet in the space of 200 yards.

The next day we stopped at Whitmore Wash, where by prior arrangement, Georgie had cans of gas packed in. We would soon be more dependent on our motor to move us in the slow river current

Words cannot describe the sensation of pitching, turning, twisting, riding the crest of the wave one minute, dropping into the depths of a trough the next. The raft buckled and turned. We headed for a high rock on which

Rafting through Lava Falls

and Lake Mead.

Most commercial raft trips today end at Whitmore Wash and are air lifted to Grand Canyon Village. Other trips terminate about 40 miles downstream at Diamond Creek where on the south side, you can drive a motor vehicle to the rivers edge.

From there on there were no more spectacular rapids. We had to provide our own excitement with water fights and floating along with the rest on our air mattresses.

We passed by another favorite departure point at Pierces Ferry but continued on to Temple Bar on Lake Mead. Dr. Bill Marlow had driven my pickup to Temple Bar as he and a friend were there fishing. We were soon on our way home. A great experience.

Horseplay on Lake Mead

XII Grandview Trail to Horseshoe Mesa

November 11-13, 1966

We had already made two trips down the Grandview Trail in 1966, but some of the scouts wanted another conditioning hike in preparation for their "fifty miler" scheduled for later in the month. We picked the weekend of November 11th to 13th. I didn't keep a record of the boys making the hike but it was most of the senior scouts of Troop 1.

Grandview Trail

Our first night on Grandview Point was bitter cold. My down sleeping bag kept me warm but I discovered that the water in my canteen was frozen when I started to make my coffee the next morning. The Grandview Trail is an easy decent and good introduction to inner canyon hiking. When we got to Horseshoe Mesa, we talked about taking the right hand fork and camping at Page Spring but ended up going down the trail on the west side of the mesa to our usual camping spot at Cottonwood Spring. Here again we looked for the trail down to the Colorado River and couldn't find it.

Grandview Trail

We had our usual dehydrated supper and evening around the campfire. As I look back on it, I think how fortunate we were that we could still have campfires. Telling stories and singing songs around a bu-gas lantern leaves a lot to be desired.

The next morning we were up and on the trail at a reasonable hour. Since this was primarily a conditioning hike, we stayed pretty well together and moved right along. There was not much traffic, in fact only a couple of groups and none on the Cottonwood Canyon Trail. We were out on top in time to have lunch and start for home.

XIII RIM TO RIM TO RIM

November 23-27, 1966

The Grand Canyon Council of the Boy Scouts of America realizing that in the Grand Canyon they had a unique place for outdoor achievement. They set up an awards program with patches to be given

Panoramic view

and affixed to the boys back packs. The first was "Rim to River"; the second "Rim to Rim"; the third "Rim to Rim to Rim". Troop 1 decided to combine the Council requirements with the National "Fifty Miler" award.

This award required the boys to hike 50 miles in a minimum of five days.

In the fall of 1966 we blocked out five days, November 23 to 27th. The group consisted of Dr. Taylor Hicks, Paul Ridenhour, Wayne and Dennis Price, Bob Cook, Twig Branch, Jim, Bob and Vic Lytle.

We left our cars at Yaki Point and went down the South Kaibab Trail to the river. We met the Dave Palmer family from Prescott on the trail. They were having sore foot problems and were only going to Phantom Ranch. Their daughter Beth who was in good physical condition and not having any foot problems asked if she could join us and hike at a little faster pace.

Left to right: Mark Burhans, Vic Lytle, Jim Lytle, Dave Palmer, Beth Palmer, Paul Ridenhour

After crossing the Colorado River, we had a brief rest at Bright Angel Campground, before hiking on to the North Kaibab Trail to the Cottonwood Campground for the night. The next day we fixed a sack lunch, left our packs there, and were on our way to the North Rim. Beth Palmer joined us again to the rim. We soon came to one of the most spectacular sights in the north south corridor of the Canyon - Roaring Springs. True to its name we heard it before we could see it. Our trail up Roaring Springs Canyon was on the opposite side from the spring and offered many photo opportunities.

Roaring Springs

There is no water on this trail and I had told everyone to fill their canteens when we were crossing Bright Angel Creek for the last time. But as usual there is always one that doesn't get the word. This time it was Twig Branch. By the time he discovered his plight, we were about a fourth of a mile past and 500 vertical feet above the stream. Twig took off like a mountain goat on the most direct route to the stream. Taylor Hicks had taken advantage of the stop to get just one more picture. I hollered to Taylor that he had plenty of time as Twig had gone down to fill his canteen. Twig thought I was calling him, that we were moving on. So here he came charging back up the hill without a drop of water in his canteen. We decided we could all share water and moved on up the trail.

About midmorning we came upon a rock slide across the trail which required some extra care in negotiating it. That was the first time we had such an encounter on one of the Parks maintained trails. As we approached the North Rim, the 7,000 foot altitude began to take its toll. We made frequent stops to get our breath. It was about lunch time when we topped out. There was about a foot of snow on the level ground. The sun was bright and the day was warm.

Some of the boys decided to melt snow to augment their water supply for the return trip. They found out that it was a slow process and that a canteen cup packed with snow and held over the fire didn't produce a quarter of a cup of water. There were days on canyon hikes that I would have given a lot for a quarter of a cup of unpolluted water.

The hike back, all down hill and without packs was a breeze. We picked up our packs at Cottonwood

Camp and hiked on to Ribbon Falls for the night which had become a favorite spot.

Saturday was not a demanding day. After a leisurely breakfast with a second cup of coffee, we stopped only to fill our canteens at Phantom Ranch. Then we started up the South Kaibab Trail until we intersected the Tonto Trail and here we made a right turn, heading west across the Tonto Plateau to

Indian Gardens

Indian Gardens. After walking into the sun all afternoon, we stopped at Pipe Spring for a rest stop. We all welcomed the shade of the cottonwood trees at Indian Gardens where we spent the night. There isn't much use trying to sleep after daybreak in a public campground. Most of our group were rummaging around in their packs by the time the sun was penetrating the inner canyon walls. After visiting with other campers and having our breakfast, we began the last ascent. We met quite a few day hikers.

I like the Bright Angel Trail better than the South Kaibab. It's not quite as steep, has water available and although it is a little longer, it has some spectacular views.

After a bowl of chili at Bright Angel Lodge, we completed our 50 mile requirement by hiking along the Rim Trail to Yaki Point and our cars.

GRAND CANYON — RIM TO RIM — MENU — <u>NO</u> CANNED FOOD
                         _{SUGGESTED}
                         1963   EXCEPT FOR MEALS ON
                                           CANYON RIM.

THURSDAY NITE :- (PREPARED IN ADVANCE) — SOUTH RIM

      FRIED CHICKEN - DEVILED EGGS - MILK - CAKE OR COOKIES

FRIDAY MORNING :- SOUTH RIM

      BACON & EGGS - ✓CANNED FRUIT - HOT CHOCOLATE*
      (MAKE SANDWICHES FOR LUNCH)

FRIDAY NOON :- PHANTOM RANCH

      ✓SPAM SANDWICHES - FRESH FRUIT - (BANANAS, APPLES OR ORANGES)
      ✓POWDERED MILK - COOKIES

FRIDAY NIGHT :- RIBBON FALLS

      ✓CHICKEN NOODLE SOUP* - HAMBURGERS (FROZEN AT START OF TRIP)
      ✓POWDERED MILK* - COOKIES   (PUT DRIED FRUIT TO SOAK)

SATURDAY MORNING :- RIBBON FALLS

      CEREAL - (COOKED OR DRY) - FRUIT - HOT CHOCOLATE*
      (MAKE SANDWICHES FOR LUNCH)

SATURDAY LUNCH :- NORTH RIM   ✓
      SPLIT PEA SOUP - SANDWICHES - MILK* - RAISINS

SATURDAY NITE :- RIBBON FALLS   ✓
      ✓CHICKEN-NOODLE SOUP* - *SWISS STEAK DINNER* - COOKIES & MILK*

SUNDAY MORNING :- RIBBON FALLS
                      *
      ✓RANCH STYLE BREAKFAST* - HOT CHOCOLATE*

SUNDAY NOON :- PHANTOM RANCH -   ✓
      ✓VEGETABLE SOUP* - *DRIED FRUIT* - MILK*

SUNDAY NIGHT :- INDIAN GARDENS   X   ✓
      CHICKEN STEW - *DRIED FRUIT* - *COOKIES - MILK*

MONDAY MORNING :-
      ✓RANCH STYLE BREAKFAST* - HOT CHOCOLATE*

* DEHYDRATED FOODS

71

GRAND CANYON - RIM TO RIM - EQUIPMENT   JIM LYTLE

WHAT TO TAKE

- ✓ YUCCA PACK OR PACK FRAME ✓
  — EXTRA LASHING —
- ✓ SLEEPING BAG — B
- ✓ QUART CANTEEN & CUP B
- ✓ FLASH LIGHT ✓
- ✓ MESS KIT & KNIFE FORK SPOON B
- ✓ DISH TOWEL OR PAPER TOWELS
- ✓ S.O.S. PADS B
- ✓ MATCHES B
- ✓ CHANGE OF UNDERWEAR B
- ✓ CHANGE OF SOCKS (2 EXTRA PAIR)
- ✓ WASH CLOTH TOWEL & SOAP B
- ✓ KLEENEX ✓ ✓ CHAP STICK B

TO LEAVE IN CAR

TWO EXTRA BLANKETS B
AIR MATTRESS B
HEAVY JACKET OR SWEATER

OPTIONAL

- ✓ POCKET KNIFE ✓
- ✓ COMPASS ✓
- ✓ CAN OPENER
- ✓ POT HOLDER
- SWIMMING TRUNKS B
- ✓ CAMERA ✓
- ✓ SNAKE BIT KIT
- ✓ FIELD GLASSES

WHAT TO WEAR

- ✓ LEVIS & SHORTS
- × LONG SLEEVE SHIRT
- TWO PAIR OF SOCKS
- ✓ HIKING BOOTS OR
    HIGH TOP TENNIS SHOES
- LIGHT JACKET
- CAP OR HAT WITH BRIM

TWIG   MARC   RIC
BADAY   JIM   PAUL

72

XIV HERMIT TRAIL TO THE COLORADO RIVER

It is hard to believe that in twelve years of Canyon hiking we had not ventured down the Hermit Trail. On the last week of March, 1967, Troop 1 decided to try it. At that time it was listed by the Park Service as an abandoned trail and not maintained.

The gradient of the trail was not physically demanding. We enjoyed replenishing our water supply from the Santa Maria Spring just a short distance down the trail. Our troop was in good shape so it took some of the strain off the scoutmaster and his assistants.

As we left Lookout Point we had a magnificent view of the Hermit Basin. The steepest part of the trail was aptly called Cathedral Stairs, then on down the switchbacks to Hermit Campground. Here we found the usual bare ground covered with trash.

One patrol decided to follow the trail down to the river but the rest of us spent time cleaning the campsite and picking out good places to bed down. It always seems to get dark in a hurry once the sun sinks behind the Canyon rim. So it was a short evening, particularly for those who had gone down to the river.

I have noticed that I can remember with quite some detail the things that have gone wrong on our canyon hikes, but when all

is going well, I am so wrapped up
in the grandness of the scenery
that I don't recall specific
happenings. This is by way of
saying we had an uneventful hike
out of the Hermit Basin and a safe
journey home.

XV North Bass Trail and Out the South Bass Trail

October 12-16, 1967

There is a difference in unmaintained trails. We had a little taste of it on a portion of our Thunder River trip. Now we were going one step further, the North Bass Trail. In October 1967, Dennis and Wayne Price, Paul Ridenhour, and I were joined by new hiking friends - Andy Tomlinson and John Ludwig. Wayne and I had added a new perspective to our advance

Muave Canyon North Bass Trail

planning on this hike. We had done an aerial reconnaissance flight of Mauve Canyon and the Powell Plateau.

Ethel and Rosa Earl Williams delivered us to the trail head at Swamp Point on the North Rim of the Canyon. Our perspective was a little different when we were on the ground up to our eyeballs in buck brush, trying to spot a rock cairn along the bank of

75

White Creek. We missed our marker for the break in the Redwall and had to backtrack to find it. Wayne told me later that he was really as concerned about our well being as at any time in our canyon hikes. When we finally found the rock cairn, we didn't see how we could have missed it. White Creek was spring fed and increased in size as we followed it. We found a quiet pool under the shade of some cottonwood trees for a lovely campsite.

View of the Colorado River from the Bass Trail

It was an easy trail to follow the next morning. We heard the roar of Bass Rapids before we saw them. That was enough to impress upon us the importance of getting across the river before being swept into the white water of the rapids.

We proceeded to our launching site about a fourth mile upstream.

There we inflated our air mattresses, secured our packs and boots on top of them and secured a hand line to our makeshift rafts to keep them from getting away if we lost our contact.

Andy Tomlinson crossing the Colorado River above Bass Rapids

We ended up almost directly across from our starting point due to a back eddy as we neared the opposite bank.

The sandy beach made an ideal campsite. The sand was warm and the sun bright. We were in no hurry to be moving on. We actually had time for a nap as well as time to explore the area.

The water was cold and invigorating. Pushing our rafts ahead of us, we headed for the opposite shore.

We found the abandoned boat of Charles Russel, August Tradje

Vic and Paul Ridenhour coming in for a landing on the south shore of the Colorado

Boat abandoned at Bass Rapids

(who took moving pictures), and a Mr. Clement. The boat was left there in 1915. It was built by Bert Loper and named the Ross Wheeler for a friend who had been killed. We were impressed by two facts. The boat was in an almost perfect state of preservation due to the warm dry climate. The level of the river must have been 25 or 30 feet above its present flow to have

been at waters edge or slightly above when it was abandoned.

We also found the south shore anchor point for a tramway across the river that had been part of Mr. Bass's mining operation.

We had not had an arduous day, so we lingered around our campfire and enjoyed the peace and quiet of an autumn evening and a beautiful starlit night.

South shore anchor point for tram

Campsite at Bass Rapids

The next morning we found the South Bass Trail to be in much better shape than the northern segment even thought it is not maintained by the Park Service.

About midmorning Andy spotted the skull and horns of a Desert Big Horn Sheep. It seemed big enough to make Boone and Crocket rating and Andy decided to pack it out. An hour or so later, he changed his mind and stashed it away to be retrieved at a later date.

The Charles Tewksbury family and the Wayne Price family were to meet us at the head of the South Bass Trail. "Chuck" had tentatively agreed to hike down the trail to meet us. We had been keeping an eye out for him but when we reached the Darwin Plateau without seeing him, we became quite concerned. Since we had not made a rendezvous point, we had no choice but to continue upward on the trail. When we reached the rim, he was waiting for us.

Redwall on the North Bass Trail

He had gone down a side trail and decided he had missed us. The ladies had prepared a picnic lunch which was a pleasant change from our dehydrated food of the last few days. It was a pleasant ending to an enjoyable hike.

We stowed our gear into the waiting cars and were soon on our way home.

John Ludwig, Vic Lytle, Dennis Price, Chuck Tewksberry, Paul Ridenhour, Wayne Price and Andy Tomlinson

XVI ELVES CHASM

April 1966, we had made a short stop at Elves Chasm on our Georgie White raft trip. One of the boatmen said that the only way into Elves Chasm was by boat. I kept looking at maps and talking with other hikers and decided that there were at least two dry land routes. A group of experienced hikers decided to go down the South Bass Trail and west on the Tonto Trail to the chasm. A long week end in November of 1969

Elves Chasm

was chosen. The group was made up of Bob Millegan, Andy Tomlinson, Ray Brown, Dr. Taylor Hicks Sr., Gerald Turley, Dave Phillips, (a Prescott College student), Bill Brann and myself. We started to put logistics together: checking road conditions, getting adequate cars and trucks for the drop-off and pick-up points, sources of water, etc.

Some family members delivered us to the trail head Thursday

evening. We didn't get an early start Friday morning, but it was pleasantly cool as we were in the shade for an hour or so. Although the South Bass Trail is not one of the Park Services maintained Trails, it gets enough traffic to keep it clear. Mr. Bass, being a miner, evidently constructed a good base when he first built the trail.

Rest stop West Tonto Trail

We had our first stop about a mile down from the rim. Here Bill Brann decided he wasn't in shape and it wasn't wise for him to continue. He said he would go back to Grand Canyon Village and return for us on Sunday. Shortly after this stop we had a pleasant surprise. A beautiful Desert Big Horn Ram appeared. He was about 25 yards off the trail and didn't seem the least bit frightened. When all the cameras started clicking, he turned first to the right side then the left and then straight on. Taylor had been taking 18 mm movies. He said, "Wait till I get my instamatic." Evidently the ram thought he said "automatic" for he turned and trotted down the canyon. What a beautiful sight!

When we reached our lunch stop, Taylor and Gerald decided they would forgo the hike to the chasm and just have a day of rest at Bass Rapids. When we reached the West Tonto Trail, Taylor and Gerald left us to continue on the river, a short distance

Rest stop West Tonto Trail

and plenty of water. The five remaining scavenged the water from their canteens to make a dry camp a little further down the trail in the vicinity of Copper Canyon.

Ray Brown developed leg cramps during the night and decided to join Taylor and Gerald at Bass Rapids. We hated to see him take off by himself, (never a good practice in Canyon hiking). But it was a fairly flat trail. He seemed well oriented and had no disabling pain if he walked slowly.

Our U.S.G.S. map showed live water in Garnet Canyon. When we arrived at the rim of Garnet Canyon, sure enough there were pools of sparkling water. When we sampled them, they were brackish brine and polluted by who knows what else. It seemed the best bet was to follow Garnet Creek down to the Colorado and hopefully go on to Elves Chasm for the night. We hadn't gone but a short distance down the creek when we came to a sheer drop off of about 100 feet with no way to climb around it. We backtracked out of Garnet Creek and started to look for another way to get down to the river.

Colorado River at Elves Chasm

Bob Milligan spotted a small rock cairn on the edge of the Inner Gorge. Sure enough there was a way to climb down to the river. Splashing around in the clear cool water was refreshing to our spirits as well as our bodies.

Retracing our steps had consumed quite a little time, so we made camp in a gathering storms a few miles short of our objective. It was dark by the time we finished supper. We all had down sleeping bags that shed the light rain pretty well but we were soaked by day break. Looking around the area we found that a few hundred yards further on there was an overhanging rock where we could have found shelter from the storm.

The day broke clear and the sun was bright. We spread out our

84

sleeping bags and other wet gear to dry while we proceeded on to the chasm. I had seen it before but it was still a thrilling sight to see the flashing stream plunging over the travertine curtain into the sparkling pool below.

We didn't have time to explore above the falls and asses the possibility of using the Royal Arch Trail, if we came this way again.

Repacking gear

Royal Arch Creek at Elves Chasm

Our bedding was dry by the time we returned to our campsite. We packed up and made it to Copper Canyon for the night.

By the time we got to the campsite at the River, the following morning, Taylor, Gerald and Ray were all packed up and ready to start up the trail to the South Rim where our transportation was awaiting us.

Taylor Hicks at South Rim

South Rim

XVII Colorado River Raft Trip with Prescott College

By 1970 Prescott College was busy changing its emphasis from a conventional liberal arts program to one that was outdoor action oriented. In June of that year, the College sponsored a float trip down the Colorado from Diamond Creek to Pierces Ferry (55 miles). The group, comprised of three college board members: Dick Wilson, Chuck Kettering, and myself, four Prescott businessmen: Bill Lerch, Doctor Jim Dickson (D.D.), Bob Hanney, Bob Fashbaugh; Prescott College Faculty: Ron Barnes, Sam Keen, John Wright, John Jansen and three or four Prescott College students. There was no hiking involved in this trip. We drove from Peach Springs right to the waters edge, inflated our rafts and were underway. Our flotilla comprised three five man rafts and one kayak. One raft was equipped

Prescott College raft trip lunch stop

with a twenty horsepower outboard motor which was for emergency use only.

The college students acted as helmsmen. The rest of us provided the paddle power. By putting in at Diamond Creek we encountered only ten of the smaller rapids and these were mostly in the 4 to 7 range of difficulty. The big ones range up to 10. We all wore life jackets all of the time and a couple of trustees swam through a number of the lesser rapids. All of us took turns using the kayak which isn't as easy as it looks.

Eventually the Canyon opens out and you are able to get away from the confines of the Inner Gorge. We made stops at Travertine Falls and at the Bridge Canyon Dam site. Travertine Falls has a similarity to the formation at Elves Chasm with the clear stream plunging over the travertine curtains that have built up over the years into a sparkling pool at its base. A planned structure, the "pumpback" power project at Bridge Canyon didn't pass the environmental test, so never materialized.

We also stopped at Separation Canyon where the Powell party split up. What a decision it was. Three of the Powell party decided to leave the river and hike out to the North Rim and were never heard from again. They were presumed to have been killed by the Indians. Recently a story came out in the Arizona Republic that perhaps the men were killed by Mormons who mistook the three for federal agents.

At this point the river flattens out and we drifted slowly down stream when we weren't paddling. It wasn't too long before we were in Lake Mead and were met at Pierces Ferry by our

Prescott College van. But we had a problem. The van was on dry ground and we were in the water with about 75 feet of mud of varying depths, left by the receding water levels of Lake Mead, between us and the van. We could walk through the mud, but there was no water to wash off with when we got to dry land. We finally made it by the use of rocks and boards and skidding the boats over the wettest parts.

In retrospect boating down the Colorado is a series of exciting events. Although there are hazards, it is more fun and games than hiking. You have more time to absorb the unique formations of the canyon walls. You also have an abundance of water which is always a problem on the trails away from the river.

XVIII Hermit Trail and out Bright Angel Trail

October 23-25,1971

I really prefer hiking in the Canyon in the spring. Generally if we have had a wet winter, the springs are all running and the days aren't too hot.

In the fall, water is not so plentiful as we found out on our Elves Chasm hike.

Troop 1, under the leadership of Dr. Jim Dickson (Dentist) chose October 23rd to 25th in 1971 for a repeat of our Hermits Trail hike, adding a little variety by taking the Tonto Trail over to Indian Gardens and out the Bright Angel Trail. It was a great pleasure to hike with Jim Dickson.

There were about ten or twelve scouts with some experience of hiking in rough country. As we started down the trail from Hermits Rest, there was no indication of what the weather would be like twelve hours later. It was a bright and sunny day and we were at the Hermit Camp by early afternoon. Dr. Dickson took part of the troop and hiked on to the river and got back about supper time.

Those who stayed in camp had been quick to pick out the most suitable places to roll out their sleeping bags and then just goofed off around camp until supper time.

There had been a cloud build-up in late afternoon, but the shower held off until we had finished supper. Though it wasn't long after supper till it started to rain and the boys who had chosen the shelter of some over hanging rocks soon had lots of company. It wasn't a good night for sleeping. No one had kept completely dry.

The morning broke bright and clear as we started east on the Tonto Trail. It didn't take us long to figure out that we were carrying extra pounds of water in our gear. We decided to remedy this when we found a bright sunny spot to spread out our bedding and clothing to dry. The solar radiation did the job and we were soon on our way with warm dry clothing and bedding. While waiting for our things to dry we explored Monument Creek. If we pass this way again, I would like to make camp there.

Since we had used up some of our time drying clothes and bedding, we had to move right along. The Tonto Trail is maintained at the 4000 foot elevation. The only thing that held us back was picking our way around Salt Creek and Horn Creek. As we moved around Horn Creek, the clouds started gathering for an afternoon shower. We had no choice but to continue across the flat to our appointed rendezvous at Indian Gardens.

The only shelter was an open air ramada with a stone floor and water running through it. However there were benches that enabled us to get our gear off the floor. Some of the boys had butane camp stoves that enabled us to heat enough food to tide us over.

It was obvious that we weren't going to have enough room for everyone to sleep under the shelter. Dr. Dickson decided to take some of the older boys and hike out in the dark. They were already soaking wet. They had flashlights for occasional use. But it was with mixed emotions that we saw them take off. But I was content to wait for daylight to bring out the younger boys.

We finally got settled down for the night and as the rain let up some of us moved out from under the shelter. About two or three o'clock, I woke up and decided I had better check on my boys. To my surprise there weren't any scouts in the area where we had bedded down. What had happened to them? All sorts of devious thoughts flashed through my mind. Could they have started up the trail on their own. Just then I heard some noise coming from the rest room. The rest room had an electric hand dryer that was activated by pressing on a button which automatically shut off after a few minutes. The boys had taped the switch open, so they had a small but efficient electric heater. The result was a warm place to spend the night. Leave it to the ingenuity of some scouts to come up with a solution to a cold wet night.

As we were to hear later, Dr. Dickson's group had no major problem. Dr. Dickson had found out there were vacancies in the Bright Angel Cabins. This offered them a short nights sleep and the rest of us a place to clean up and dry out the following morning when we reached the rim.

As usual the boys will remember this hike long after they have forgotten some of the hikes that went off without a hitch. It was memorable to me for another reason. It was the first time I had ever had a parent "chew me out" about the treatment of her son on a hike. Her gripe was about my decision to stay at Indian Gardens rather than hike out in the rain at night.

XIX PARIA CANYON

We chose May 1973 to hike the Paria Canyon from U.S. 89 in Utah to Lees Ferry in Arizona. There were four of us: David Lincoln, President of Bagdad Copper Co.; Andy Tomlinson, Prescott City Manager; Dr. Taylor Hicks, Dentist; and me.

Although the Paria River technically is not a part of the Grand Canyon, it is one of the major tributaries along with the

Paria Canyon

Little Colorado that furnishes most of the silt in the Colorado River. Since one has to walk in the water most of the way, retracing our steps to return to our cars on U.S. 90 did not appeal to us. Ralph Bilby, (President of the Babbit Trading Company) came to our rescue. He arranged to have the manager of the Babbit store in Page drop us off at the head of the trail in Utah and pick us up at Lees Ferry.

This trail is under the supervision of the B.L.M. We were expected to file a hike plan before we started down the trail but there wasn't anyone at the mobile office to check us in.

Taylor Hicks, Andy Tomlinson, David Lincoln start of the trail to Paria Canyon

There wasn't anything spectacular about the country there so we decided to proceed through the hilly terrain and make camp when we reached the narrow part of the Canyon. As near as we had been able to determine, there hadn't been any flood waters through the canyon for over a year. But there were still enough springs feeding the canyon to keep a few inches of water in the stream bed all the way to the river. It was a completely new experience. Instead of the limitless vistas of the Grand Canyon, we had confining sandstone walls that rose for hundreds of feet in height on either side of us and only 15 to 20 feet wide.

Campsite

We found one place where there was a sandbar slightly higher than the stream bed which gave us a little breathing space to make camp. There was a small stream that came down over a rock and made an ideal shower bath. Along the streams edge there was an elaborate sand castle that we found out later was made by some Prescott College students over a year before. The next morning it wasn't too long before we came to a side canyon or Buckskin Gulch.

That was even narrower and deeper than the main stream bed. We walked up it to a point where it was necessary to get wet. We didn't know what lay ahead, so we turned back. There was one place you could reach out and touch the sides of the gulch and not see the sky. At another point, we could look up about 40 feet and see a log around two feet indiameter jammed between the sides of the gulch by a flood.

Buckskin Wash

Logs jammed by a flood

That was reason enough not to schedule a Paria hike during the rainy season.

As we came out of the "narrows" we soon saw the trail leading to the Wrather Arch. It couldn't be compared to Rainbow Bridge but was worth the hike up there.

The last days hike was through rolling hills to Lees Ferry where we found our friend from Babbits, fishing the time away. We took him back to Page, had a bite to eat, and were on our way home.

Wrather Arch

XX NANKOWEAP TRAIL AND OUT THE HOPI SALT TRAIL

April 25-29, 1974

In the spring of 1974, April 25th to 29th to be exact, a group of five: Dr. Taylor Hick Sr., Andy Tomlinson, Ray Brown, Roxie Webb Jr., and myself decided that we wanted to explore the Nankoweap Trail at the east end of the Canyon. It also would serve as a survey for a future fishing trip for trophy size rainbow trout in the Nankoweap Rapids.

Hopi Salt Trail

Ethel and Jean Thompson provided transportation to the North Rim of the Canyon. We had left Taylor's car at the head of the Hopi Salt Trail, our ultimate destination. We left U.S. 89 and followed a primitive road through the Buffalo Ranch to the end and made camp.

We bid the ladies farewell and they returned to Wahweap Lodge at Lake Powell.

We were still about a mile and a half from the North Rim. The Nankoweap Trail wasn't that easy to follow. In fact we had a hard time finding the trail head. The next morning as we started up a ridge of Saddle Mountain and approached the north rim, there were a myriad of trails. We got on one leading us off to the southwest and finally decided that this trail was leadingus toward Point Imperial. Retracing our steps, we found a piece of flagstone laying in the trail at the canyon's edge inscribed with N.T. (Nankoweap Trail) on it. Taylor was not feeling well so we took a rest stop. He told me later that he would have turned back at that point had there been any transportation available, but we had passed the point of no return. Another consideration was the availability of water. Nankoweap is a dry trail. The only water you have is what you carry in until you get to the creek.

Andy was leading the way as we started down. Following him was like following a Big Horn Sheep picking his way along narrow ledges and talus slopes. About noontime we got off on a game trail that necessitated a short back track along the foot of Saddle Mountain. The views from the north side of the canyon are as awe inspiring as ever, because the 2000 foot difference in elevation gives it something of an overview of the various mesas and view points. By the time we reached Tilted Mesa the trails ups and downs began to take its toll. Taylor, Ray and I decided to call it a day. As we were preparing to make camp, Roxy and Andy decided to continue on. They soon came to a point where they could see Nankoweap Creek. They yelled for us to join them and camp along the creek. But our bodies were too weary to pack up and move. We joined them for breakfast the next morning.

The trek along the creek with the sheer canyon walls opening out to the Nankoweap Delta was worth the strain of the previous day.

Our original plan was to swim across the river in the quiet water above the rapids. We had experimented with this operation above the Bass Rapids without any problems. As luck would have it, Hatch Brothers (river runners) had pulled in for a rest stop and a chance to explore some prehistoric cliff dwellings in the area. When the rafters heard our plans, they offered to ferry us across the river. We didn't have to take a vote to determine whether to accept the offer, the water temperature being about 50 degrees.

Hatch Brothers raft at Nankoweap

We were now in Marble Canyon. There wasn't much of a view, but it was relaxing to have the river nearby. Shortly after being deposited on the south shore, we stopped for lunch. There was no trail as we walked along the beach. Our only inconvenience was the tamarack jungle which had grown up since the Glen Canyon Dam controlled the scouring action of the high waters.

These thickets presented a real problem. They grabbed at your packs and your clothing; they even managed to pull my fly rod out of my pack without my being aware of it.

When we stopped for the night, it was a real treat to have a refreshing dip in the river. We didn't need the soothing noises of the stream to put us to sleep. It was about 3,000 foot elevation at the river so the days were warm and the nights cool. The weather was perfect.

The following day we arrived at the Little Colorado a little before lunch time, right on schedule. I was expecting a murky-muddy stream. Instead it was a beautiful turquoise blue, very much like Havasupai Creek. We stripped off for a swim and were just getting our clothes back on when a five man raft appeared with a lone male at the oars or so we thought.

He had a female companion with him who was soaking up the suns rays without a stitch of clothing to inhibit her. They were soon followed by another raft with only three men aboard. There was a large stone outcropping that divided the river bank into two semi-private beaches. We finished dressing, had lunch, donned our packs and started up the Little Colorado. The trail passed right through their little campsite and there was the naked lady stretched out beside the trail. We all exchanged "Howdy's" as we continued on our way. Although we all had cameras, no one recorded this for our memoirs.

In our preliminary plans we were relying on the Little Colorado for our drinking water. We found one small spring and even that was quite salty.

About midafternoon four and a half miles upstream, we came to a travertine formation that had been formed by a highly mineralized spring that had built up a domed shaped formation at the rivers edge that was still depositing minerals for its continued growth. This is the famous "Sipapu". According to legend the Hopi people emerged from the earth at this spot. We must have been among the last white men to visit this spot as now the Hopi People with the cooperation of the National Park Service have made it off limits to backpackers, tourists, and all but the Native Americans.

Sipapu

We stopped for the night at the mouth of Salt Trail Canyon. The next morning we had a choice of water supply, neither of which was very good.

We could use halogen tablets and drink river water or go back to the last spring. We decided to go back to the spring as we thought we had plenty of time. We had misunderstood the difficulty of the Hopi Salt Trail. Even though the Hopis had been using it for centuries it was not what you would call a maintained trail. There were numerous rock slides.

The combination of progressive dehydration from drinking our brackish water soon took its toll. Taylor and I were exhausted. We did what we could to lighten our packs. Taylor was into tin can cookery at this time and they were the first to go. My eating utensils joined them in a shallow grave (so as not to litter the canyon). Excess weight was calculated in ounces. We didn't count the items we disposed of, but it helped.

As we continued climbing, the trail got steeper causing us to go on all fours at times. In one of the rough spots, a loose boulder came tumbling down hitting Roxie in the leg. The leg immediately began to swell. We thought it might be broken. In spite of the pain, Roxie decided to push on. None of us had enough strength to be of much assistance.

We finally made it out of Salt Canyon to where we had left Taylor's station wagon. I never knew that fresh water could taste so good. Taylor vowed that was his last Canyon hike. I didn't make any such vow, but I voted it the most devastating. Roxie's leg injury proved to be only a severe bruise.

XXI Tanner Trail to the Tonto Trail to the Hance Trail and out Grandview Trail

November 8-11, 1974

By the fall of 1974 we had forgotten about the trials and tribulations of the Hopi Salt Trail. We decided to continue our exploration of the trails in the east end of the Canyon. On Armistice Day weekend, November 8th to 11th Bob Schuster, newspaper reporter; Andy Tomlinson, Prescott City Treasurer; and I put together a hike down the Tanner Trail, to where we pick up the Tonto Trail and follow it to Hance Creek and out the east Grandview Trail.

We drove to the head of the Tanner Trail and made camp. It was a cold night and in the morning none of us wanted to crawl out of our sleeping bags. We had a leisurely breakfast and were on the trail by eight o'clock. The Tanner is a dry trail so each of us carried a half gallon canteen of water. It was a rather cool day with some cloud cover. Thus we had no problems of dehydration. The trail was not demanding, in fact almost boring.

We reached the Colorado River in late afternoon and made camp on a gentle slope to the south of the Tanner Rapids. In following the river the next morning, we were anticipating some drainages that would force us to work our way up to the head of these side canyons in order to proceed down stream.

They would be time consuming and tiring. Instead we chose to

105

take to the river and float around the mouth of the drainages. I believe the first one was Escalante Canyon. We inflated our air mattresses, tied our clothing, boots and packs to the mattress, secured a hand line to the make shift raft as a safety measure, should we loose our hold on the mattress. I was first into the water and was it cold! I lost no time in getting around the point and on shore again.

Thank goodness it was a warm day. However at our second canyon detour, that same afternoon, it was getting a little chilly, downright frigid in the water.

As soon as I reached shore, I put on all my clothes including my down jacket. I was shaking so much I couldn't light a match to build a fire. It was a classic case of hypothermia. Thank goodness at that time, it was still possible to build camp fires from the abundant driftwood. I would never have gotten warm over a small gas cooking flame. We hadn't had a long hike but it was good to crawl into a down sleeping bag and get warm.

The next day we used our float technique to pass another drainage which put us at Hance Rapids by early afternoon. We met a family group (the first hikers we had seen in four days) that had just come down the'new' Hance Trail. We were tempted to exit by this trail but decided to continue with our plans to go out the east Grandview Trail primarily because we knew we had a known source of water at Page Spring where we camped the night. There really wasn't any campground. All we needed was a place to roll out our sleeping bags beside the trail. We didn't have to worry about other hikers as most of them preferred the maintained park campgrounds. We spent the daylight hours that were left exploring the remains of a mining operation that had been abandoned many years ago.

The next morning, Andy and Bob were anxious to experience the Grandview Trail. It is not a difficult trail and although it is not maintained by the Park Service, it is one of the most heavily used trails outside the central corridor. It is only three miles from Horseshoe Mesa to the South Rim so we were out in time for lunch.

XXII BOUCHER TRAIL TO THE COLORADO, THEN THE WEST TONTO TRAIL

November 8-11, 1975

Armistice Day had become a popular weekend for Canyon hiking. So to avoid the crowds, Andy Tomlinson and I put together a hike on the lesser hiked Boucher Trail. Joining us was Andy's son, Danny who in 1975 was making his first canyon overnight. Andy had invited Dwight Steinbaken of the League of Cities and Towns, whose office was in Phoenix, plus Bob Schuster, and Ray Brown.

Thursday night we bedded down at Hermits Rest. Friday morning was sunny and bright as we followed our plans to hike down the Hermit Trail. A short time later we reached the Dripping Springs Trail and on to the spring and the head of the Boucher Trail.

Since the Boucher is a dry trail, we filled our canteens and were on our way. About midmorning and in the vicinity of Columbus Point, we stopped for a rest. Danny decided he had enough and was ready to turn back. His father informed him that we had reached the point of no return. Because the Boucher Trail was not too clearly defined, we had to give more attention to our footing and keep our eyes peeled for rock cairns. We made it through the Redwall without any difficulty and made camp near the Boucher Rapids. The rapids provided background music for our slumber.

In all our canyon hiking, we had never put our backpacks out of reach of nocturnal marauders. However my pack was generally within reach when any disturbance occurred. I had not been asleep long when something awakened me. In the pale of the moonlight, I could see something moving at the foot of my sleeping bag. I reached for my flashlight which revealed a skunk trying to get something out of my pack. The light also revealed that I was looking down the business end of his spraying equipment. I quickly retreated to the limited protection of my sleeping bag. Mr. Skunk decided that whatever he might find wasn't worth the effort and he waddled off down the canyon. None of the other packs were molested, nor did any of the other hikers awaken.

We got an early start Saturday morning following the Tonto Trail, crossing a number of drainages, each carrying the remains of precious stones - slate, agate, sapphire, turquoise and rubies. Serpentine Canyon was the last one that presented any real problem. We finally called it a day at Bed Rock Tank. As planned, we met Wayne Price and some other Prescott hikers who had arrived there on time.

Next morning, we all hiked out the South Bass Trail. This was about our fifth trip on the Bass Trail so we felt right at home. It had been a very enjoyable hike.

XXIII KAIBAB TRAIL TO PHANTOM RANCH WITH THE LINCOLN FAMILY

January 6-8, 1978

When I was hiking with David Lincoln in Paria Canyon, he mentioned that his family would like to take a hike in the Grand Canyon. It had been a couple of years since we discussed this so I was quite surprised when Dave called me and said the Lincoln family were planning a two day hike to Phantom Ranch and wondered if I would like to go with them. Because they were staying at the ranch, backpacks were not necessary. I rode up to the Canyon with the Lincoln boys. Joan (Mrs. Lincoln) had some back problems and didn't feel she should hike but rode a mule. The rest of us walked down Bright Angel Trail.

I had heard stories of trophy trout being caught in the Colorado River so I packed my fishing gear to give it a try.

We got settled in our rooms. Dave, Joan and I were in a cabin; the boys were in the dormitories. There was still some daylight left so I took my fishing rod and walked down to the river. I fished in the rapids where Bright Angel Creek comes into the Colorado but didn't have any luck. I had been using a Rapella lure then changed to flies and tried Bright Angel Creek. Still no luck. So back to the lodge.

We had a pleasant evening visiting in the lodge. The following morning the hikers waited till Joan was aboard her mule to start our hike out the

South Kaibab Trail. The mules
were ahead of us and out on top
before we got to the rim. It was a
pleasant family excursion.

XXIV Indian Gardens

I have always thought that Canyon hiking had to be backpacking and overnight camping. But in June 1979, John and Evelyn Hollowell (our Congregational minister and his wife) asked me about hiking in the Grand Canyon. He had a hard time fitting something into his schedule so we planned a day hike to Indian Gardens and back. Jennifer Hollowell and her boyfriend joined us.

I generally like to hike some less demanding trails with my hiking companions before taking them into the Canyon. However the Hollowells were avid tennis players and appeared to be in good physical condition.

We left Prescott about 4:00 a.m. and had breakfast in Williams. Hiking permits were not required for short day hikes so we packed a light lunch and started down the Bright Angel Trail. The thing I found most unusual were the number of people on the trail. There was one man pushing a child in a stroller. Saw one young lady in a bikini and wearing high heels. Those who had come from the river were dragging a little and generally asked how much further it was to the rim.

When we reached Indian Gardens, the shade of the cottonwood trees was quite welcome. While John, Evelyn and I rested, Jennifer and friend hiked out to Plateau Point and back. They were setting such a fast pace, we didn't see much of them on the trail.

The Hollowells didn't find it so difficult hiking in, but they had a few more rest stops on the way out. Evelyn said she wasn't ready to try it again. We were on the rim in time to see a typical Grand Canyon sunset. After having dinner at Bright Angel Lodge, we started back for Prescott. Needless to say we were all very tired.

XXV KAIBAB TRAIL TO PHANTOM RANCH - A FISHING TRIP

December 9-11, 1979

In December, 1979 I joined a hiking and fishing group of 8 or 10 put together by Chuck Fears to hike in and out of the Kaibab Trail and stay at Phantom Ranch. We drove up in his motor home and one car. Three or four of the group were avid golfers and thought they were in good physical condition but found out otherwise. Backpacks were not necessary since we were not camping out. Most had day packs and a sack lunch.

It was quite a different experience from my early Canyon hikes where the youngest was seven years of age and all were in top physical shape. On this hike the oldest, Rudy Lemke was probably 70 and also having knee trouble.

In the evening we had steaks, gin rummy, and beer in place of dehydrated foods and campfire stories.

The following day was not programmed. Some hiked to Ribbon Falls, some were occupied with their cameras, and some of us went fishing. On the way to the river, I met a little girl with a single trout in her dip net. Its head was hanging out one side, its tail out the other. We found out later that it weighed 10 pounds. She had caught it in Bright Angel Creek on salmon eggs. I had excellent luck catching four rainbows and two German browns in the Colorado. I had noticed some likely looking riffles along Bright Angel Creek during the morning, so I gave them a try on the way back to the cabins. I had a little luck, but no keepers. The lodge had a deal, that if you cleaned the fish, they would wrap them in foil and freeze them for you.

When we gathered for dinner that evening, it was determined that Randy was not in any shape to hike out. We contacted the Park Ranger to see if he could get a mule for him to ride. This presented a logistics problem of getting a mule down to the ranch with no reservations for an extra night at the lodge. The final solution was to have a helicopter come in, if the Ranger determined that Randy really was disabled. The Ranger gave it his ok and Jim Bard decided to go out with him. This solved one of my problems as I really hadn't looked forward to packing out seven pounds of fish.

Jim put them with his pack so they went out by helicopter and into the freezer in the motor home.

The lodge had made lunches for those who wanted them. There were several degrees of proficiency in hiking out. Two long legged men made it out in a little over two hours; several of us stopped at Cedar Ridge for lunch and a little rest. It was a great hike, and nice to relax in Chucks motor home on the way back to Prescott.

116

XXVI DIAMOND CREEK-A FISHING TRIP

December 3-5, 1980

The increasing popularity of hiking in the Grand Canyon has made it necessary to make plans about a year in advance. Chuck Fears made reservations at Phantom Ranch for December of 1980 for the usual group of Prescott retirees and Navy buddies. The increase in the number of people using the central corridors, Bright Angel and Kaibab Trails had put a strain on the sanitary facilities. The Park Service closed the Bright Angel Campground and Phantom Ranch until the situation could be corrected. This made it necessary to cancel our plans and look to next year. Glenn Goddard had been planning to join our fishing group. We had been hiking once a week in order to get in shape and Glenn couldn´t see all that conditioning go to waste. So we decided to go further down the Canyon and try the fishing at Diamond Creek. This is the only access to the Colorado between Lee´s Ferry and Pierce´s Ferry where you can drive a vehicle right to the edge of the Colorado.

We took Glenn´s motor home and it was well that we did. I have never seen such a dirty campground. It was not a long drive from Prescott so we had a little time for some fishing that afternoon. There was a little water in Diamond Creek so we did a little fly fishing where the creek flows into the Colorado. We had no luck and decided to wait till morning and try some lures in the

deeper part of the river. As is
generally the case, places that are
easily accessible do not produce
many fish. We picked our way up
stream along the shore but didn´t
have any luck. We were back to
the camper by noon. After a short
nap, we tried to find some
suitable holes down stream. There
really were not very many good
spots. We didn´t try bait fishing.
Perhaps that is what the fish
wanted.

We spent the rest of the day
exploring some side canyons. I
enjoyed seeing some different
views of the Canyon in spite of
catching no fish. It was a most
relaxing weekend.

XXVII KAIBAB TRAIL TO PHANTOM RANCH A FISHING TRIP

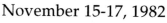

t was November of 1982 before we could get reservations for our Prescott hiking and fishing group at Phantom Ranch. The composition of the group had changed. Two ardent fishermen who were attracted by the stories of the trophy trout coming out of Bright Angel Creek were Paul Hicks and Waldo Bast. Waldo, who was a retired school teacher and long time scoutmaster, was approaching his 80th birthday and had been with us on one of our Rainbow Bridge hikes, wanted to give it a try.

We started down the south Kaibab Trail and by the time we reached the Cedar Ridge rest area, it was obvious that Waldo was not going to make it. A Park Ranger helped him to make the decision to turn back. Paul stashed his pack and helped Waldo with his. Paul was in excellent shape and after he had settled Waldo on the South Rim, he ran back down the trail and soon caught up with the rest of us.

While talking with Paul about fishing, we made a little wager as to who would catch the biggest fish. With this incentive, Paul went on ahead and was fishing away by the time we got to the river. I still had to go up to the ranch (about a half mile), shed my pack, get my fishing gear together and go back to the river. It wasn't long before Paul had landed a beautiful rainbow about twenty five inches long. I didn't see how

119

I could beat that but I kept on fishing. Paul decided he had enough for one day and went back to the cabin. I was about to give up when I hooked a beauty. By the time I landed it, I was ready to save some for tomorrow too. When I got back to the lodge, all our gang were gathered around for "Happy Hour" admiring Paul's fish. They wanted to see mine. They still had some "ohs" and "ahs" left. Mine turned out to be twenty-five and a half inches long and a little over five pounds. We still had another day!

Vic and his five pound trout

The day dawned bright and clear. Paul started up Bright Angel Creek which ran by the lodge.

Chuck and two or three others took the Clear Creek Trail knowing full well that they wouldn't make it to the creek. Others walked down stream on the Colorado for some photography. I followed Bright Angel Creek down to the Colorado, wetting a line now and then when I saw a likely looking pool. I followed the pipe line footbridge and fished form the south shore for awhile. I had one great strike just below the bridge, but that was all. Didn't do much better above the bridge.

After lunch and a little nap, I went back out and caught

two four pound rainbows and one
big brown. Paul hadn't done any
better, so I won the wager.

The next morning we were on the
trail by eight o'clock. Chuck came
to my assistance by packing out
two of my fish. I wouldn't part
with my big one. There were
many speeds of walking and more
rest stops, but we all made it out
on time. We said good-bye to
some of our California friends
who were not returning to
Prescott. The rest of us were soon
on our way home. It's a fishing
trip I'll never forget.

XXVIII Bright Angel Trail to Phantom Ranch

December, 1983

There had been some snow at the Grand Canyon by the time we had scheduled our annual hiking and fishing trip in December of 1983, but a call to Phantom Ranch confirmed our reservations and that the trails were open.

Some of the group hadn't been down the Bright Angel Trail, so those who had crampons for their boots went that route. My nephew, Wally Patterson from Phoenix who had joined us for this trip, and Len Barker kept an eye on me.

South Kaibab Trail

The trail was icy in spots but we didn't experience any trouble. The snow gave a new perspective to the Canyon's peaks and valleys. The trail was clear by the time we got to Indian Gardens so we took off our crampons. As we proceeded down the creek, we came across three deer grazing near the trail. They came up on the trail and walked along between us when the canyon was very narrow. But as it became wider, the deer continued their grazing. It wasn't long until we reached the river and found some boys fishing. We rested awhile in the information shelter and read about the alluvial action on the Canyon. From there on the trail runs right along the rivers edge until you reach the bridge and the Inner Gorge is all you can see.

My knees started to give me trouble requiring more rest

Confluence of Pipe Creek and the Colorado River

stops than usual. I told Wally and Len to go on ahead. I would get there in due time. Those who had come down the South Kaibab Trail had been at Phantom Ranch for quite awhile. Chuck Fears was concerned about my physical condition and came back on the trail to see if I needed any help.

We had our usual round table after dinner and made plans for the next days activities. I decided to forgo fishing to take the Clear Creek Trail with some of the hikers. There were some spectacular views looking across the Inner Gorge to the Tonto Plateau with just enough clouds to accent the spires and valleys. We were back in time to compare notes with the others on our days activities.

The third day I decided to fish Bright Angel Creek to see if I could catch some browns. With the four fish limit, one could be selective in what they kept.

The four I kept were nothing to
brag about.

As it turned out, this was my last
Canyon hike, but had been one of
my most relaxing, a pleasant
combination of fishing and hiking,
visiting, and napping. I had taken
time to enjoy the ever changing
vistas and the delicate colors
varying from one minute
to the next.

When I first started to put
together these memoirs, it was
with a sense of accomplishment.
As I look back I concur with
Psalm 8, verse 4 "What is man
that thou are mindful of him."

In Fond Memory

Vic Lytle

Born: Sept. 25, 1911 in Coldwater, Kansas
Died: Dec. 24 1995 in Prescott, Arizona

Bright Angel Creek

Vic finished this book in 1994 and wanted to have it published for hiking friends and family. The photos are all his except the cover picture which was taken by Dr. Jim Lytle.

CANYON MEMORIES

This book was published in July of 1997
by TecnoArte Editorial S. A. de C. V. in Mexico City.
The pages are printed on Xerox Image Series LX 90 gram paper using
Palatino Type of 9, 12, 18, and 36 points.
Edition of 60 copies. This is part of our "Books on Demand" project so any
amount of additional copies can be made at anytime.
Design and layout: Ma. Aurora Arellano Saucedo
Photo imaging: Rafael Tapia Yáñez.